Copyright © 2024 Alisa Lively

The contents and illustrations may not be reproduced in any form without written permission from the publisher or author, except as permitted by U.S. copyright law.

Book Cover by Ade Chintya

Illustrations by Ade Chintya

ISBN: 979-8-9911861-1-7

Silent Books Publishing
www.silentbookspublishing.com
Baltimore, MD

It's the Small Things that Count

It's the Small Things that Count

Written By
Alisa Mauk Lively

Illustrated by
Ade Chintya

Megan was a wonderful, small girl who made a big impact. She had many differences, but she did small things that made her extraordinary to everyone around her.

She spent lots of her time at her mom's job, West Virginia Wesleyan College. There, Megan was a dreamer and a giant.

Megan was beautifully petite, about four feet tall. She was vibrant, with a sparkle in her green eyes and an amusing belly laugh that could make anyone happy.

Her big heart, full of love and unique charm, made a memorable impression on everyone.

Megan had dark brown hair and loved to style it in a high ponytail with a colorful scrunchie.

Megan wore sparkling earrings and loved to dress for the season or holiday. She loved to sport crocs. Everything she wore had to match perfectly!

Megan had a condition called ring chromosome 18 that disrupts the ordinary course of physical development. This condition made her much shorter than average, but that didn't discourage her from spreading joy everywhere she went. Hearing, speaking, reading, and writing were difficult for Megan, but she never let that discourage her.

Every month, she received infusions at her doctor's office, which made her stronger and more resilient than one could imagine. Even though her infusions could cause discomfort, Megan was tough. She never complained.

Megan embraced her life with passion and her condition never caused her to doubt herself. From birth, she had a hip issue that caused her to walk with a limp, yet she moved through Wesleyan lively and determined to give grace and receive it.

Megan spent most of her days crafting. She enjoyed making friendship bracelets, unique beaded structures, and colorful animals. With a heart full of generosity, she gifted all her crafts to family and friends in the campus offices and the surrounding community.

Megan loved crafting, but her true passion was Special Olympic Sports! She was a fierce and powerful competitor. She had incredible stamina in practice and was a much greater powerhouse on competition days.

Megan earned ribbons and bronze, silver, and gold medals in many Olympic sports. She played basketball, bowling, bocce, cheerleading, and competitive walking.

Her team spirit was infectious! The sound of cheering support from family on the sideline during games gave her the push she needed to be a star on and off the field.

Megan never let an ache or pain slow her down. Looking at her, you could not tell that her body was hurting every day. She hopped right in and ensured her teammates did their parts, stayed in line, and had their supplies.

Megan was a beacon of light to West Virginia Wesleyan College and never missed out on joining in on the fun. She was a proud community volunteer. She volunteered at the cafeteria entrance, counting students during meal time and guiding them to the proper exits when they finished eating.

The staff always thanked her with chocolate chip cookies! She often helped with supplies at campus events, contagiously spreading her joy. Bingo nights were the best!

Megan's big heart touched the lives of everyone around her. The Wesleyan community cherished her friendship and kindness.

Megan's story gradually became a big part of Wesleyan's culture. Her legacy lives on in the memories she left behind and the people she impacted. Huge high-fives, squishy hugs, and everlasting laughs are imprints of Megan's love.

Megan was big on bravery, commitment to joy, and being herself, but she understood that with family and friends, it's the small things that count. She was a true dreamer and giant. Megan would want everyone to know that any small gesture makes a big difference!

Please pay it forward for Megan!

About Author

Alisa Mauk Lively is a strong advocate for Special Olympics West Virginia and Special Olympics Upshur County. She advocates for children and adults who are mentally challenged to have year-round events of a variety of Olympic style sports, where athletes are given opportunities to develop physical fitness, demonstrate courage, experience excitement and simply just make new friends!

Lively has worked in higher education for 40 years and enjoys engaging her college students in volunteerism for Special Olympics, a teaching moment for both the student and the athlete.

She was blessed to be the mother of Megan, to whom this book is dedicated, for thirty-three wonderful years and reaped the rewards of Megan's altruism through the eyes of a perpetual child.

Lively hopes you enjoy teaching your children to see the world through all lenses, especially the lens of a special-needs child.

About Illustrator

Ade Chintya is an Indonesian based Illustrator. She has been creating illustrations for Children's books since 2016. Her illustrations have been published in various print and web media. For more information, **visit www.adechint.com.**

www.ingramcontent.com/pod-product-compliance
Lightning Source LLC
Chambersburg PA
CBRC090058100526
44582CB00013B/181